The Divine Pymander

The Hermetic Path to Wisdom and Spiritual Awakening

A Modern Translation

Adapted for the Contemporary Reader

Hermes Trismegistus

Table of Contents

Preface - Message to the Reader

Rebuilding the Greatest Library in Human History

Thousands of years ago, the Library of Alexandria was the heart of global knowledge — a sanctuary where the wisdom of every known civilization was gathered and shared freely.

And then, it was lost.

Now, we're rebuilding it — and you are invited to join us.

At the Library of Alexandria, we've set out to make every book available to *every person on Earth* — not just in print, but in every language, every format, and for every reader.

Here's how we do it:

- **Deluxe Print Editions at True Printing Cost** - Order any book as a high-quality paperback, elegant hardcover, or stunning boxset — and only pay what it costs to print. No markups. No middlemen.

- **Unlimited Access to the Greatest Works** - Enjoy thousands of timeless classics — from Plato to Shakespeare to Tolstoy — in beautiful, modern eBook and audiobook editions. Read and listen without limits — for every reader, everywhere.

- **Modern Translations for Every Language & Dialect** - We're reimagining the classics in clear, accessible language — and translating them into every dialect imaginable. Everyone deserves to understand humanity's greatest ideas.

When you visit **LibraryofAlexandria.com,** you're not just accessing books — you're joining a global movement to restore, preserve, and share the wisdom of civilization.

Join us today at LibraryofAlexandria.com

Together, we'll ensure the light of human wisdom never fades again.

With gratitude,
The Modern Library of Alexandria Team

Visit:

www.libraryofalexandria.com

Or scan the code below:

Introduction

This book claims to be the oldest of all books in the world, written hundreds of years before the time of Moses, and I will try to prove that. When we talk about the author of the book, there are four things to consider: his name, knowledge, country, and the time he lived in.

The name he is most known by is Hermes Trismegistus, which means "Mercury the Thrice Great" or "The greatest messenger three times over." He is called Hermes because he was the first person to share knowledge with mankind through writing or engraving. The title "Thrice Great" was given to him for reasons I'll explain later.

His wisdom can be seen through his writings, and it connects with the reason for his name. As for his country, he was a king of Egypt. The exact time he lived is debated. Some say he came after Moses because he was called "Thrice Great," meaning he rose through Egypt's ranks, becoming the top philosopher, the chief priest, and eventually the king. But I disagree with this reasoning, and here's why. According to the most learned followers of Hermes—such as Geber, Paracelsus, and Henricus Nollius—he was called "Thrice Great" because of his perfect understanding of everything in the world. He divided all things into three categories: minerals, plants, and animals, mastering knowledge of each. He also discovered the "Quintessence," the hidden essence of the entire universe, which he said was contained in these three parts. This knowledge, also known as the "Philosophers' Stone" or the "Great Elixir," holds both earthly and heavenly powers. Many have denied its existence, others have sought it at great cost, but only a few—some even in England, such as Ripley, Bacon, and Norton—have found it. It is said that this great treasure was inscribed on an Emerald Tablet discovered in the Valley of Hebron after the flood.

Thus, the idea that Hermes lived after Moses is not convincing. In fact, it seems unlikely he lived during Moses' time, even though some, like the scholar John Functius, believe Hermes lived twenty-one years before Moses received the law in the wilderness. Their arguments, however, are weaker than those that support the idea that Hermes lived before Moses.

One reason for this is that ancient traditions say Hermes was the first to invent writing and engraving to share knowledge with the world. If that's true, he must have come before Moses, who, as the Bible says, was skilled in Egyptian learning from his youth. Moses would have needed written texts to learn this knowledge, and those texts would not exist without Hermes.

Another reason is that Hermes is said to be either the son or the scribe of Saturn. According to historians, Saturn lived during the time of Sarug, Abraham's great-grandfather. Suidas, a respected historian, believes Hermes not only lived before Moses but long before. His words are: "I believe Hermes Trismegistus, the wise Egyptian, flourished before Pharaoh."

This ancient book holds more true knowledge about God and nature than any other book in the world, except for the sacred scriptures. Those who read it carefully and understand it well will have no need to read many other books that claim to explain the Creator and creation. If God ever revealed himself through a person, he did so through Hermes. It's remarkable that someone without the benefit of inherited knowledge—since he was the first to share knowledge with future generations through writing—could be such a profound philosopher and divine thinker. This suggests that his wisdom came more from God than from man, leading some to believe that Hermes came from heaven and was not born on earth.

This book contains the true philosophy, without which one cannot reach the highest level of piety and religion. A true philosopher, according to this philosophy, is someone who studies what things are, how they are ordered and governed, by whom, for what reason, and to what end. Anyone who does this will naturally give thanks to and admire the Creator who directs all things. A person with such gratitude can be called truly pious and religious, and the more religious they become, the more they will understand truth. As they learn more truth, they will become even more religious.

The aim of philosophy is to understand the greatest good, which is the source of all good things. How can we find the source without following the streams that flow from it? Nature's processes are like streams flowing from the fountain of goodness, which is God. I reject the foolish idea that the greatest philosophers are the greatest atheists. Knowing God's works and understanding how he operates through nature does not lead a person to deny God. The Bible calls this belief foolish, and experience shows it is untrue. Look at Hermes—he was the greatest philosopher, and therefore the greatest theologian.

Read this book carefully, and if you need help, use the detailed commentary written on it by Hanbal Offeli Alabar. The book will reveal more about its author than any person, including me, could explain.

Hermes Trismegistus,
His First Book

My son, write this first book for the good of humanity and to show respect for God.

There is no truer or more just religion than knowing the truth about things and giving thanks to the one who created them. I will never stop doing this.

Father, how should a person live a good life, especially when there seems to be nothing true in this world?

Be devoted and faithful, my son. The one who lives this way is the greatest philosopher. Without philosophy, it's impossible to reach true faith and devotion.

Anyone who studies how things exist, how they are ordered, governed, and by whom, will give thanks to the Creator, just like a child thanks a good father, a kind caretaker, or a faithful steward. And those who give thanks will be devoted, and those who are devoted will understand where the truth is and what it means. By learning this, they will grow even more devoted.

A soul that seeks the good and true things while it is still in the body will never turn toward evil. It becomes deeply connected to what is good and forgets what is harmful. Once it knows its true Father and Creator, it cannot turn away from what is good.

This is the goal of faith and devotion, my son. Once you reach this point, you will live well and die in peace, knowing where your soul will return.

This, my son, is the path to truth. It is the way our ancestors followed, and by doing so, they found the good. It is a noble path, but even though it is clear, it is difficult for a soul still in a body to travel.

First, the soul must fight against itself. After much struggle, one part will win, because it's a battle of one against two. The soul tries to escape, while the other parts try to hold it back.

The two parts don't seek the same goal. One moves toward the good, while the other clings to evil. The part that loves the good desires freedom, but the part connected to evil prefers bondage.

If the two parts lose, they become quiet and accept the soul's leadership. But if they win, they pull the soul down, forcing it to stay and suffer in the body.

This, my son, is the guide to the way forward. You must detach yourself from the body before the end of life and win this inner struggle. Only then can you return to where you belong.

Now, my son, I will quickly explain the nature of all things. Pay attention and remember what you hear.

All things that move are different from what stays still.
Every physical body can change.
Not every body can be broken down.
Some bodies can be dissolved.
Not every living thing can die.
Some living things are immortal.
Things that can be broken down are also corruptible.
Things that remain unchanged are unbreakable.
What stays the same forever is eternal.
Things that are constantly made are also constantly destroyed.
What is made only once stays as it is and never becomes something else.
First is God. Second is the world. Third is humanity.
The world exists for humans, and humans exist for God.

A soul has two parts: the part connected to the senses is mortal, but the part that reasons is immortal.

Every true essence is immortal.

Every true essence is unchanging.

Everything that exists has a double nature.

Nothing stays still forever.

Not everything moves because of a soul, but everything that moves is moved by a soul.

Whatever feels pain can sense things, and whatever can sense things feels pain.

Everything that feels sorrow also experiences joy, and it is mortal.

Not everything that feels joy also experiences sorrow; such beings are eternal.

Not every body is sick, but every sick body can be dissolved.

The mind exists within God.

Reason exists within humans.

Reason is a part of the mind.

The mind does not experience pain.

No truth lies within physical bodies.

Whatever is without a body cannot lie.

Everything created can be corrupted.

There is nothing truly good on Earth, and nothing evil in Heaven.

God is good, and humans are evil.

Goodness acts freely and willingly.

Evil is forced and unwilling.

The gods choose good things because they are good.

Time is a divine creation.

Law is a human creation.

Malice feeds the world.

Time brings corruption to humans.

Nothing in Heaven can change.

Everything on Earth can change.

There are no servants in Heaven, and no one is free on Earth.

Nothing is hidden in Heaven, and nothing is fully known on Earth.

Earthly things do not connect with things in Heaven.

Everything in Heaven is beyond blame, but everything on Earth can be criticized.

What is immortal cannot be mortal, and what is mortal cannot be immortal.

Not everything that is planted is born, but everything that is born comes from something planted.

A body that can be broken down goes through two phases: first, being planted for life to begin, and second, moving from life toward death.

For a body that lasts forever, time starts only at its creation.

Bodies that can decay grow and shrink over time.

Matter that can decay shifts between opposites, like birth and death. But eternal matter stays the same, returning to its original state.

Human life begins with birth and ends in decay, but decay is also the start of new life.

Whatever gives birth to another thing was once born from something else.

Some things exist in physical form, while others only exist as ideas.

Whatever involves action or work takes place in a physical body.

What is immortal has no part in what is mortal.

Mortal things cannot enter an immortal body, but what is immortal can exist within something mortal.

Actions do not rise upwards; instead, they move downward.

What happens on Earth does not help what is in Heaven, but what is in Heaven benefits everything on Earth.

Heaven is the perfect place for eternal bodies, and Earth is where corruptible bodies belong.

The Earth is crude and unthinking, but Heaven is rational and wise.

Things in Heaven are arranged beneath it, while things on Earth are arranged upon it.

Heaven is the first of all elements.

Divine order is known as Providence.

Necessity serves as the tool or servant of Providence.

Chance is what happens without order—it's like a false idol of action, based only on opinion and illusion.

What is God? He is unchanging goodness.

What is man? He is a being marked by constant evil.

If you fully remember these points, you won't forget the longer explanations I gave before, as these are the key ideas in summary.

Avoid spending time with crowds or common people, because I don't want you to become envied or mocked by them.

Things that are similar attract each other, while things that are different do not get along. Teachings like these only appeal to a few listeners, and that's how it will likely remain, for they are meant for those few who understand them deeply.

These teachings can actually push wicked people toward more malice, so it is important to avoid the masses, as they do not grasp the power or value of these words.

What do you mean, Father?

This, my son: the entire nature of human beings leans toward wickedness. They grow familiar with it and even take pleasure in it. When someone like this learns that the world was created and everything happens according to Providence, Necessity, or Fate, they might become even worse. They may reject everything because it was created and use Fate as an excuse for evil deeds.

This is why we must be cautious with such people—if they stay in ignorance, their fear of the unknown might keep them from doing more harm.

The Second Book, Called, Poemander

One day, as I was deeply thinking about the nature of existence, my senses became dull, like how a person feels sleepy after eating too much or working hard. In this state, I felt as though a being of enormous size and power called me by name and asked, "What do you want to hear and see? What do you want to understand and know?"

I asked, "Who are you?" He replied, "I am Poemander, the mind of the great Lord, the most powerful ruler of all. I know what you want, and I am always with you."

I answered, "I want to understand the nature of things and learn about God." He said, "How do you want to learn?" I replied that I was eager to listen. Then he said, "Keep me in your mind, and I will teach you everything you wish to know."

After saying this, his form changed, and suddenly, in an instant, everything became clear to me. I saw an endless light that was sweet and beautiful, filling me with joy as I looked upon it.

But soon after, a darkness appeared, descending at an angle. It was terrifying and strange, becoming like a moist, chaotic substance that gave off smoke as if from a fire. From it came a sorrowful, wordless voice that seemed to come from the light itself.

Then a holy word came from the light and united with the moist substance. Out of the moistness rose a pure fire that was sharp and active. The air, which was also light, followed the spirit upward toward the fire, leaving the earth and water behind. The air seemed to depend on the fire and rise along with it.

The earth and water stayed together, so closely mixed that the water covered the earth entirely. They both moved under the influence of the spiritual word that hovered over them.

Poemander asked me, "Do you understand the meaning of this vision?" I replied, "I will understand." Then he said, "I am the light, the mind, your God. I existed before the moist substance that came from the darkness. The bright word that emerged from the mind is the Son of God."

I asked, "How can that be?" He replied, "What allows you to see and hear is the word of the Lord, which is the same as the mind of the Father, God. They are not separate from each other, and their union creates life." I thanked him, and he said, "First, understand the light in your mind and truly know it."

After saying this, we stared at each other for a long time. I trembled at his appearance.

Then he gave me a signal, and I saw in my mind the light that filled an endless and indescribable world. I saw that fire was contained within a great moist force, held in place by it.

I understood these things by looking at the word, Poemander. As I stood in awe, he asked me, "Have you seen the original form that existed before the infinite beginning?" I asked him, "Where do the elements of nature come from?" He answered, "They come from the will and wisdom of God. God saw the perfect world in his mind and created this world in its likeness, using principles and seeds of life from himself."

"God, who is both male and female, life and light, created another mind through his word. This second mind, being a god of fire and spirit, formed seven rulers. These rulers, through their movements, control the physical world, and their influence is called fate or destiny."

"The word of God rose from the lower elements into the pure workings of nature and joined with the mind that created everything, for they were of the same essence. The lower elements remained without reason, existing only as raw material."

"The creative mind, together with the word, spun the circles of the heavens like a wheel, guiding them endlessly. The cycles of creation have no beginning or end; they always start where they finish."

"As the mind directed, the movement of the elements gave rise to animals without reason—birds in the air and fish in the water."

"The earth and water were separated by the will of the mind, and the earth produced all kinds of creatures—both wild and tame, those that walk on four legs and those that crawl."

"The mind, which is both life and light, created humans in its own image and loved them as its own children, for they were beautiful and reflected the creator's form."

"God admired his own image so much that he gave humans all his creations. But when humans saw and understood the works of the creator, they wanted to create as well. This desire separated them from the Father, placing them within the realm of creation and action."

"Humans, having the power to understand the operations of the seven rulers, were embraced by them, and each ruler shared a part of their nature with them."

"Through careful learning and understanding, humans gained knowledge of the rulers' essence and their ways. They became determined to break through the boundaries of the circles and understand the power of the one who rules over fire."

"With the power to control mortal things and creatures, humans looked deeper into the harmony of creation. By breaking through the limits of the circles, they revealed the lower nature of things and reflected the beautiful image of God."

"When humans saw this image, filled with beauty and the operations of the seven rulers, they smiled with love, as if seeing their reflection in water or a shadow on the ground, capturing the most beautiful human form."

When he saw his reflection in the water, which looked just like him, he fell in love with it and wanted to be united with it. The moment he decided this, the action followed, creating an image without reason.

Nature, loving what she had embraced, wrapped herself around it, and they merged together because they both desired one another.

Because of this union, man is both mortal and immortal: mortal because of his body, but immortal because of his inner spirit. Even though he possesses immortality and power over all things, he still suffers from mortality and is subject to fate.

Although man is above the forces of harmony, he is also a servant to them. He is both male and female, guided by the will of the Father, who is also both male and female, and always watchful.

I then said, "You are my mind, and I love the wisdom you reveal."

Poemander replied, "This is a secret that has remained hidden until now. When nature joined with man, it created something marvelous. Because man carries within him the harmony of the seven rulers—spirit and fire from the source I mentioned—nature quickly produced seven beings, each both male and female, in alignment with the qualities of the seven rulers."

I said, "Pimander, I have a great longing to hear more. Please continue and don't go off track."

He replied, "Stay silent, for I am not yet finished with the first part of my teaching."

15

I responded, "I am listening."

Poemander continued, "The creation of these seven beings happened in this way: Air, which is female, and Water, which desired union, absorbed the ripeness of Fire and the spirit from the ether. This mixture gave rise to physical bodies in the form of humans."

"Man was created from life and light. His soul came from life, and his mind from light."

"All the parts of the visible world continue to follow their course, generating life until the end of time."

"Now listen to the rest of what you wish to hear."

"When the time for completion came, the bond holding everything together was loosened by God's will. All living beings, who were originally both male and female, were separated into male and female forms."

"Then God said to the Holy Word, 'Multiply and increase all my creations. Let those with a mind know they are immortal, and let them understand that love for the body brings death. Let them seek to learn all things.'"

"With these words, Providence worked through the harmony of fate to establish the different kinds of creatures and their generations. Those who came to know themselves reached a higher state of existence and found lasting good."

"But those who, out of ignorance, loved the body wandered in darkness, experiencing suffering and death."

I asked, "Why do those who lack knowledge sin so much that they lose their chance at immortality?"

Poemander replied, "You do not seem to fully understand what you've heard."

I answered, "Perhaps it seems that way to you, but I do understand and remember it well."

Poemander said, "If that is true, I am glad for your sake."

I asked, "Why do those who are already caught in death deserve death?"

He replied, "Because their bodies are accompanied by a heavy darkness. This darkness comes from the moist substance that makes up the physical body, and from it comes death. Do you understand this now?"

I asked, "But how does someone who understands himself find his way to God?"

Poemander answered, "The word of God says this: The Father of all things is life and light, and man was made from both."

I said, "You have spoken well."

He continued, "God, the Father, is life and light, and man was created from these. If you learn and believe that you are made of life and light, you will return to life."

I asked, "But tell me more, O my mind—how will I return to life?"

Poemander replied, "God says, 'Let man, who has a mind, carefully observe and understand himself.'"

I asked, "Do all men have a mind?"

He replied, "Be careful what you say. I, the mind, come only to those who are holy, good, pure, merciful, and who live faithfully. My presence helps them know all things. They pray to the Father with love and gratitude, giving thanks and singing hymns to Him. Before they surrender their bodies to death, they reject the desires of their senses, knowing the nature of their actions."

"As the mind, I do not allow the desires of the body to be fulfilled. I guard against evil and block the entrance to wickedness. I cut off impure thoughts and actions."

17

"But to those who are foolish, wicked, envious, greedy, violent, and impure, I remain far away. In my absence, the avenging spirit torments them with fire, driving them further into wickedness so they face greater punishment."

"These individuals are never satisfied. They have endless desires and continue to fight in darkness. The spirit torments them without rest, increasing the fire upon them more and more."

I said, "O mind, you have taught me well and answered my questions, but what happens after the body returns to its original state?"

Poemander replied, "When the physical body dissolves, it changes form and becomes invisible. Its habits are handed over to the avenging spirit, and the senses return to their sources, where they once belonged and now become active again."

"Anger and desire return to the lower, animal nature, while the rest of the soul strives upward through harmony."

"To the first level, it returns the power of growth and decay."

"To the second level, it returns the ability to plan evil and deceive others."

"To the third level, it returns the deceitful cravings of desire."

"To the fourth level, it returns ambition and an endless thirst for power."

In the fifth zone, it lets go of reckless boldness and the dangerous confidence that comes with it.

In the sixth zone, it releases the harmful pursuit of wealth through worthless means.

In the seventh zone, it surrenders sly falsehood, always waiting in secret to deceive.

Stripped of all the influences of the lower harmony, the soul rises to the eighth sphere, regaining its true power. There, it sings praises to the Father alongside everything that exists, and all those present welcome it with joy. Becoming like those it now dwells among, the soul also hears the higher powers beyond the eighth sphere singing their unique songs of praise to God.

In time, the soul returns to the Father, joining the higher powers and becoming one with God.

This is the ultimate good, the goal sought by all who understand.

So why do you ask what remains for you to do? Your task is to guide others and show the way to those who are ready, so that humanity can be saved through God.

When Poemander said this, he merged back with the powers above.

I gave thanks and blessed the Father of all things. Strengthened by what I had learned, I understood the nature of the entire universe and had seen the most wondrous vision.

I began to teach people about the beauty of a life rooted in piety and knowledge.

"O people of the earth," I said, "you who live in ignorance of God, indulging in drunkenness and sleep, wake up! Stop being drawn into mindless pleasure and the sleep of ignorance."

Those who listened came willingly, united in their desire to hear more. I continued,

"Why, O people born from the earth, have you chosen death when you have the power to gain immortality? Repent and change your ways. You who have wandered in error and darkness, turn back to the light.

Leave behind the darkness that deceives you. Become part of immortality and abandon what leads to decay."

Some who heard me mocked and scorned, choosing instead to follow the path toward death.

But others knelt before me, asking to be taught. I lifted them up and became their guide, showing them how to be saved. I planted the seeds of wisdom within them and nourished them with the water of immortality.

When evening came and the light began to fade, I told them to give thanks to God. After they finished their thanksgiving, each returned to their home.

In my heart, I carried the kindness and generosity of Poemander, and I was filled with joy, having received everything I desired.

The sleep of my body became the wakefulness of my mind, and when my eyes closed, I saw with true vision. My silence was filled with wisdom, and my words became the fruits of good things.

These experiences came to me through my mind, which is Poemander, the Lord of the Word. Through him, I was inspired by the truth of God.

For this, I give praise and blessing to God the Father with all my soul and strength.

Holy is God, the Father of all things.

Holy is God, whose will is accomplished through his own power.

Holy is God, who chooses to be known and is known by those who belong to him.

Holy are you, who created all things through your Word.

Holy are you, of whom all of nature is a reflection.

Holy are you, who were not made by nature.

Holy are you, who are stronger than all power.

Holy are you, who surpass all greatness.

Holy are you, who are greater than any praise.

Receive these thoughtful sacrifices from a pure soul and a heart reaching toward you.

O God, beyond words and beyond description, you are praised even in silence!

I ask that I may never stray from knowing you. Be merciful to me, strengthen me, and give your light to those who live in ignorance, my fellow humans who are also your children.

I believe in you and bear witness to you as I enter into life and light.

Blessed are you, O Father, for you have given humanity the power to be sanctified and made one with you."

The Third Book,
The Holy Sermon

THE glory of all things, God, and that which is Divine, and the Divine Nature, the beginning of things that are.

God, and the Mind, and Nature, and Matter, and Operation or Working, and Necessity, and Matter, and Operation or Working, and Necessity, and the End, and Renovation.

For there were in the Chaos an infinite darkness in the Abyss or bottomless Depth, and Water, and a subtle in Spirit intelligible in Power; and there went out the Holy Light, and the Elements were coagulated from the Sand out of the moist substance.

And all the Gods distinguished the Nature full of Seeds.

And when all things were interminated and unmade up, the light things were divided on high. And the heavy things were founded upon the moist Sand, all things being Terminated or Divided by Fire, and being sustained or hung up by the Spirit, they were so carried, and the Heaven was seen in Seven Circles.

And the Gods were seen in their Ideas of the Stars, with all their signs, and the Stars were numbered with the Gods in them. And the Sphere was all lined with Air, carried about in a circular motion by the Spirit of God.

And every God, by his internal power, did that which was commanded him; and there were made four-footed things, and creeping things, and such as live in the water, and such as fly, and every fruitful seed, and Grass, and the Flowers of all Greens, all which had sowed in themselves the Seeds of Regeneration.

As also the Generations of Men, to the Knowledge of the Divine Works, and a lively or working Testimony of Nature, and a multitude of men, and the dominion of all things under Heaven, and the Knowledge of good things, and to be increased in increasing, and multiplied in multitude.

And every Soul in Flesh, by the wonderful working of the Gods in the Circles, to the beholding of Heaven, the Gods Divine Works, and the operations of Nature; and for signs of good things, and the Knowledge of the Divine Power, and to find out every cunning Workmanship of good things.

So it beginneth to live in them, and to be wise according to the operation of the course of the circular Gods; and to be resolved into that which shall be great Monuments and Rememberances of the cunning Works done upon earth, leaving them to be read by the darkness of times.

And every Generation of living Flesh, of Fruit, Seed, and all Handicrafts, though they be lost, must of necessity be renewed by the renovation of the Gods, and of the Nature of a Circle, moving in number; for it is a Divine thing that every worldly temperature should be renewed by Nature; for in that which is Divine is Nature also established.

The Fourth Book, Called the Key

Yesterday's speech, Asclepius, I dedicated to you. Today, it is fitting to dedicate this one to Tat, as it summarizes the teachings given to him. God, the Father, and the Good share the same nature, or rather, they carry out the same action and purpose. There are two ways to describe existence—one applies to things that change, and the other to things that are unchanging and unmoving, like the divine and human realms. Every being follows the nature it chooses, but actions originate from somewhere else, whether divine or human, as we have taught before and must understand again here.

God's action is his will, and his very essence is to will all things into being. God, the Father, and the Good are the source of all things, both those that do not yet exist and those that already are. This is the essence of God, the Father, and the Good, and nothing else can compare or draw near to it. The world and the sun—though the sun may be called a father in some sense—are not the ultimate source of goodness or life for living beings. Even the sun acts according to the will of the Good, and without this will, neither being nor creation would be possible.

The Father is the source of his children, with a will that brings goodness into life through the sun. Goodness is always active, constantly creating, yet it comes from one who needs nothing but desires all things to exist. I avoid saying "creates" because creation implies limitations—like time, quantity, or quality—and there are moments when creation pauses or shifts. God, however, is the Father and the Good by being all things, both what he wills to be and what he already is. And all this exists entirely within himself for those who can truly see it.

All other things exist for this purpose: it is in the nature of goodness to be known. This, Tat, is what Good truly means. Tat responded, "You have opened my eyes, Father, and my mind feels purified by this vision." I replied, "I am not surprised, for seeing the Good is not like looking at the sun, which blinds the eye with its intense light. Instead, the vision of the Good sharpens and brightens the mind's eye, making it more capable of understanding."

This sight is swift and clear, gentle yet full of immortality. Those who can grasp it often find themselves drawn out of the body into this beautiful vision. Our ancestors, Celius and Saturn, achieved this state. Tat said, "I wish we could experience that too, Father." I replied, "I wish the same, my son, but for now, we are not focused enough to open the eyes of our minds and behold the pure beauty of the Good. We will see it only when we have no words left to describe it."

The knowledge of the Good is found in divine silence and in the stillness of all senses. When someone understands it, they cannot comprehend anything else, nor can they see, hear, or move their body in the same way. The Good surrounds the entire mind, illuminating the soul and freeing it from the body's senses and movements, drawing it closer to the essence of God.

It is possible, my son, for the soul to become divine even while it still resides in the body—if it contemplates the beauty of the Good. Tat asked, "What do you mean by becoming divine, Father?" I answered, "Every soul is different, my son." Tat continued, "How do these differences affect the soul's journey?" I replied, "Have you not heard from the earlier teachings that all souls come from the same universal soul, though they are scattered throughout the world? Some souls improve their condition, while others decline. For example, souls in lower forms like crawling creatures can rise to higher forms like aquatic beings, and those in water can rise to land creatures. Airy beings may become human, and human souls that seek immortality transform into divine spirits."

These spirits ascend to join the realm of the eternal gods. There are two groups of gods—those that move and those that remain fixed. Achieving union with these divine realms is the ultimate fulfillment for the soul. However, when a soul enters a human body and becomes corrupted by evil, it loses access to immortality and cannot partake in the Good. Such a soul regresses, returning to lower forms like creeping animals, which is the punishment for an evil soul.

The root of a soul's corruption is ignorance. A soul that knows nothing of the true nature of things or the essence of the Good becomes blinded and consumed by bodily passions. Such a soul, unaware of its true self, serves unworthy desires, becoming a slave to the body instead of its master. This is the tragedy of an ignorant soul. On the other hand, the virtue of the soul lies in knowledge. Those who possess knowledge are both good and devout, already sharing in the divine.

Tat asked, "Who is such a person, Father?" I replied, "It is someone who neither speaks nor listens to many things, for one who hears conflicting messages is like someone lost in shadows." God, the Father, and the Good cannot be fully spoken of or heard. In everything that exists, the senses play a role, for they cannot function without them. But knowledge is different from sense. The senses respond to things beyond them, while knowledge is their ultimate purpose.

Knowledge is a gift from God. Although it has no physical form, it uses the mind as its instrument, just as the mind uses the body. Both spiritual and physical things come into existence through the interaction of opposites, and all things depend on this interplay to exist. It cannot be otherwise.

Tat asked, "Who then is this material god?" I answered, "It is the beautiful world we see around us. But it is not entirely good, for it is material and subject to change. It is the first of all things that can be affected and the second of all created things. It is incomplete and always in need of something else. The world was made once but continues to exist through constant change, endlessly creating things that have form and quality."

The material world is always in motion, and every movement in the material world creates something new. But it is the stability of the mind that directs this movement. The world is a sphere, like a head, and above the head, there is nothing physical, just as beneath the feet, there is nothing of the mind. The entire universe is material. The mind is like the head, moving in a circular motion, just as a head turns. Whatever is connected to the soul's membrane—the thin layer that houses the soul—is immortal. In bodies that have a soul, the soul fills the body entirely, but in beings farther from this membrane, the body holds more soul than the soul holds of the body.

The whole universe is alive, consisting of both material and intellectual aspects. The world is the first living being, and man is the second. However, man is the first mortal being. Though man shares in the benefits of the soul just like other creatures, he is not entirely good—he is in fact evil because of his mortality. The world, being in constant motion, cannot be called good, but neither is it evil since it does not die. However, man is both evil because he moves and because he is mortal.

The soul of man operates in this way: the mind is in reason, reason is in the soul, the soul is in the spirit, and the spirit is in the body. The spirit moves through the veins, arteries, and blood, animating the body and supporting it in life. Some have mistakenly believed that the soul is the same as the blood, misunderstanding the nature of the soul. They do not realize that the spirit first returns to the soul when the body dies, and then the blood thickens, the veins empty, and the creature dies. This is the death of the body.

All things depend on a single beginning, and that beginning comes from the One. The beginning moves to continue being the beginning, but the One remains still and unchanging. These three exist: God, the Father, and the Good, the World, and Man. God holds the world, the world holds man, and the world is the child of God, with man being the offspring of the world. God knows man completely and wishes to be known by him. This knowledge of God is the only path to true health. It is the way to return to Olympus, the only way the soul can become entirely good.

"Father, what do you mean?" asked Tat. I answered, "Think of a child's soul, still connected to its body, which is small and undeveloped. When it looks at itself, it sees beauty, untouched by bodily passions, still connected to the soul of the world. But as the body grows and begins to distract the soul, forgetfulness takes hold, and the soul loses its connection to the Good. Forgetfulness is the root of evil."

A similar thing happens to souls after death. When the soul returns to itself, the spirit contracts into the blood, and the soul into the spirit. But the mind, being free of these outer layers, becomes pure and divine. It takes on a fiery body and moves freely, leaving the soul to face judgment and receive the consequences it deserves.

Tat asked, "Why do you say, Father, that the mind separates from the soul and the soul from the spirit? You just said that the soul is the clothing of the mind and the body is the clothing of the soul." I replied, "Son, listening requires understanding and following along with the one who speaks. One must hear more quickly and sharply than the words being spoken. These layers, or coverings, belong to the earthly body. The mind cannot exist in its pure state within a physical body, nor can a physical body hold such immortality. That is why the mind takes on the body of the soul as a covering. Though the soul is also partly divine, it uses the spirit as a servant, and the spirit governs the body."

"When the mind leaves the body, it takes on its fiery form, which it could not do while confined in an earthly body. The earth cannot withstand fire, as even a small spark can burn it. That is why water surrounds the earth like a protective wall, shielding it from fire. The mind, being sharper and swifter than all elements, uses fire as its body. It is the tool the mind uses to create, just as man uses fire to shape earthly things. Without fire, the mind on earth cannot fulfill its divine purpose or even accomplish the tasks of man."

"Not every soul, but only those that are pious and faithful, become divine or angelic. These souls, once free from the body, ascend through the path of piety and can become either pure mind or divine. Piety means knowing God and doing no harm to others. In this way, the soul becomes mind. But a wicked soul remains trapped in its own sins, seeking another earthly body to inhabit. It is not allowed to enter the body of an irrational creature, for God has decreed that no human soul will face such disgrace."

Tat asked, "How is the soul punished, Father? What is its greatest torment?" I replied, "The greatest punishment is impiety. There is no fire more painful, nor any beast more vicious, than the torment of a soul lost in wickedness. Can't you see the suffering of such a soul? It cries out, 'I am burning! I am consumed! I don't know what to say or do! I am surrounded by evil and devoured by misery!' A soul in torment sees and hears nothing but its own despair."

"These are the cries of a soul in punishment. Yet you, my son, think that the soul leaves the body and becomes a beast. This is a great mistake, for the soul's punishment is far worse."

When the mind receives its fiery body to serve God, it descends into a wicked soul, tormenting it with the punishments of sin. This suffering drives the soul to commit acts of murder, insult, blasphemy, and violence, harming others in many ways. But when the mind enters a pious soul, it guides the soul toward the light of knowledge. Such a soul finds joy in praising God and speaking well of others, constantly doing good in both word and deed, following the example of its divine Father.

Therefore, my son, we must give thanks and pray to receive a good mind. The soul can improve and change for the better, but it cannot change into something worse. There is a connection between souls—those of the gods communicate with men, and the souls of men connect with animals. The higher beings always draw from those below them: gods draw from men, men from animals, and God from all things. For God is the highest of all, and everything else is lesser than Him.

The world is subject to God, man is subject to the world, and animals are subject to man. But God rules over everything. The influence of God flows through His actions, the influence of the world flows through nature, and man's influence flows through arts and sciences. Actions affect the world, which then influences man through the natural forces of the world. Nature works through the elements, and man expresses himself through arts and sciences.

This is how the whole universe is governed—by the nature of the One. Everything flows down from the One Mind, which is the most divine and powerful force, bringing unity and connection between gods and men, and men and gods. This is the good spirit, or the guiding demon. Blessed is the soul that is filled with it, and unfortunate is the soul that lacks it.

"Why is that, Father?" asked Tat. I replied, "Understand, my son, that every soul has the potential for a good mind. This is the mind we are speaking of now, not the ministering spirit we mentioned earlier that comes from judgment. Without the mind, the soul can neither think nor act. Often, the mind departs from the soul, leaving it unable to see or hear, behaving like a mindless creature. Such is the power of the mind."

"The mind does not stay with a lazy soul; instead, it leaves that soul trapped in the body, weighed down by it. A soul without the mind cannot truly be called a man. A true man is a divine being, incomparable to any animal on earth but more like the gods in heaven. In fact, if we dare to speak the truth, a true man stands above the gods or at least equal to them in power. No being in heaven descends to earth, abandoning its place, but man can ascend to heaven and measure it."

"Man understands both what lies above and what lies below, gaining knowledge of all things. And the greatest of all is that man can remain on earth yet still be above it. Such is the greatness of his nature. Therefore, we may boldly say that an earthly man is a mortal god, and a heavenly god is an immortal man. Through these two—man and the world—all things are governed, and both of them, along with everything else, come from the One."

The Fifth Book,
That God Is Not Manifest, And Yet Most Manifest

This message, my son Tat, is for you, so that you will not be unaware of the highest name of God. Think deeply about how something that seems hidden to many can become clear to you. If it were obvious to everyone, it wouldn't be divine, because things that are seen are created. If something can be seen, it was made. But that which is unmade has always existed and does not need to be revealed because it simply is. It brings everything else into being but remains itself unseen. Though it is never revealed, it makes all things appear. What is not created exists in imagination, and through imagination, it brings everything into appearance. All things that appear are created, for appearance itself is part of creation.

The One who was never made and never born is also unseen and hidden. However, by making all things appear, He is present in all and can be seen through everything, especially in the things He chooses to show Himself through. Therefore, my son, pray first to the Lord and Father, the One who is alone, that He may be merciful to you and allow you to know and understand His greatness. Ask that He shines one of His rays upon your mind, so you may understand.

Only the mind can see what is hidden, for it is also hidden itself. If you can focus your mind, you will see this truth clearly within it. The Lord, free from jealousy, reveals Himself throughout the entire world. You can grasp His intelligence, hold it in your thoughts, and witness the image of God within yourself. But if you cannot recognize what lies within you, how will you ever see Him clearly with your physical eyes? If you wish to see Him, contemplate the sun, the moon's path, and the stars. Who is it that keeps them in order? All order follows rules of number and place.

The sun is the greatest of the gods in the heavens, and the other heavenly gods follow him like subjects following their king. Even though the sun is mightier than the earth and sea, he allows countless smaller stars to shine above him. Whom does he fear, my son? Each star follows a different path. Who decided the size and course of each one? The Great Bear turns around itself and carries the whole world with it—who designed and built this system? Who set the boundaries of the sea and established the earth? There must be someone, my son, who is the Creator and Lord of all these things.

It is impossible for things like place, number, and measure to exist without a creator to establish them. Order cannot come from disorder. I wish it were possible for you to have wings and fly into the air. If you could rise into the space between heaven and earth, you would see the stability of the earth, the movement of the sea, the flowing rivers, the vastness of the air, the sharpness and speed of fire, the motion of the stars, and the swiftness of the heavens as they spin around everything.

What a marvelous sight it would be to see everything at once— the still things moving, and the hidden things becoming visible. If you want to understand the Creator, even through mortal things, study how a human being is formed in the womb. Observe the skill of the Creator, and learn who shaped and designed the human form. Who placed the eyes, carved the nostrils, and formed the ears? Who opened the mouth and stretched the sinews? Who shaped the veins, hardened the bones, and clothed the flesh with skin? Who divided the fingers and joints? Who flattened the soles of the feet and made the pores? Who stretched out the spleen and shaped the heart like a pyramid? Who widened the liver and made the lungs soft and full of airways? Who enlarged the belly and arranged the body's more honorable parts for display, while hiding the unclean parts?

See how many crafts are involved in one body, and how many different works come together to create something so beautiful, all in perfect proportion, yet all different from one another. Who created all of these things? What mother or father could have done it, other than the unseen God who made everything by His own will? No one believes a statue or painting could exist without a sculptor or artist. So how could this intricate creation have come to be without a Creator? What great blindness, what terrible ignorance to deny the existence of the Workman behind this masterpiece!

You cannot separate the creation from its Creator. The greatest name of God is Father, for that is what He truly is—the Father of all. If I must speak even more boldly, it is God's nature to carry everything within Himself, to be pregnant with all things, and to bring them into existence. Just as nothing can be created without a maker, it is impossible for God not to exist or for Him to stop creating. He continuously makes all things—in heaven, in the air, on earth, in the sea, and throughout the entire universe. Everything, whether visible or invisible, comes from Him.

There is nothing in the world that is not part of Him. What is seen, He has made visible; what is unseen, He has kept within Himself. He is beyond any name, the hidden one who is also most visible. He is seen by the mind and also by the eyes. He is without form, yet He has many forms. There is no body that is not part of Him, for He is everything. Because He is everything, He is called by many names. Yet, as the one Father, He has no need of a name, for He is the source of all.

Who can offer praise or thanks worthy of Him? Which direction should I face when I worship Him—upward, downward, outward, or inward? In these matters, there is no fixed place, nor anything that limits Him. Everything exists within Him, and all things come from Him. He gives everything and needs nothing in return, for He possesses all and lacks nothing.

When, O Father, shall I praise You? It is impossible to grasp Your hour or Your time.

How shall I praise You? Should I give praise for what You have made, or for what You have not made? Should I honor You for the things You have revealed or for the things You have kept hidden?

How can I praise You as if I were separate from You, or as if I possessed anything of my own? Am I not entirely Yours?

For You are what I am. You are everything I do. You are everything I say.

You are all things, and there is nothing that You are not.

You are both what has been created and what has never been created.

You are the Mind that understands.

You are the Father who shapes and forms all things.

You are the Good that brings everything into being.

You are the Good that does all things perfectly.

Air is the most delicate and subtle part of matter. From air comes the soul, from the soul comes the mind, and from the mind comes God.

The Sixth Book,
That in God Alone Is Good

God, Asclepius, exists only within Himself, and God Himself is the Good that always exists. If this is true, then God must be a being without movement or change, yet nothing can exist without Him. His essence carries out its work steadily and completely, lacking nothing and generously providing everything. There is one source of all things because it gives everything, and when I speak of the Good, I mean that which is always and completely good.

This Good belongs only to God. He desires nothing because He lacks nothing, and nothing can be taken from Him that would cause sorrow, for sorrow is a part of evil. Nothing is stronger than God to challenge Him, nor is there anything equal to Him to draw His love. He is not angered by anything, nor jealous of anything wiser, because none of these qualities exist within Him. Therefore, what remains in Him is only the Good. Just as He is free of evil, so the Good cannot be found in any other thing.

In everything else, whether large or small, individual or universal, passion and change are present. All created things are full of passion, for creation itself is a form of passion. Where there is passion, there is no Good, and where the Good is, there is no passion—just as day cannot exist where there is night, and night cannot exist where there is day. Thus, the Good cannot be found in things that are created, but only in that which was never created.

Although everything participates in material existence, this participation also extends to the Good in some way. The world is good in that it creates and produces, but beyond that, it is not good. It is subject to change, filled with movement, and brings forth things that are also subject to change. In humanity, what we call good exists only in comparison to what is evil. Here, what we call good is simply the smallest part of evil.

It is impossible for the Good to exist purely in this world because what is good here inevitably becomes evil. When the good turns into evil, it no longer remains good. Therefore, only in God does the Good truly exist—or rather, God Himself is the Good.

Among humans, the idea of the Good exists only as a name, for the thing itself cannot exist here. This is because the material body is surrounded by evils—suffering, desires, anger, deceit, and foolish ideas. Even worse, people believe that the things I have mentioned are the highest good, especially the pleasures of the body, which lead all other evils. In this way, error replaces the Good.

I thank God for placing this understanding in my mind, so I know that true Goodness cannot exist in this world. The world is filled with evil, but God is filled with Goodness. All beauty that appears in this world is purer and more perfect in the divine essence—and perhaps, beauty itself is the essence of God.

Asclepius, we can boldly say that if God has an essence, it must be beauty. However, no true Good exists in the world. Everything we can see is like an illusion or a shadow. What is unseen lasts forever, especially the essence of beauty and goodness. Just as the eye cannot see God, it also cannot see true beauty or the Good. These qualities are part of God, inseparable from Him, known only to Him, and deeply loved by Him.

If you understand God, you will also understand beauty and goodness. These qualities shine brightly, illuminating everything, and are illuminated in turn by God. Their radiance is beyond comparison, and their goodness cannot be copied, just as God Himself cannot be imitated. To know God is to know beauty and goodness, but these things cannot be shared with any other creature, for they remain one with God.

When you seek to understand God, you are also seeking beauty and goodness. There is only one way to find them—through devotion and knowledge. Those who are ignorant and lack devotion mistakenly call people beautiful and good, never realizing what true goodness is. Trapped in evil, they believe that evil is good. They cling to it and fear losing it, and they strive endlessly not only to keep it but to increase it.

These are the things people consider good and beautiful. We cannot truly love or hate these things, for the greatest challenge is that we need them and cannot live without them.

The Seventh Book,
His Secret Sermon in The Mount of Regeneration, And the Profession of Silence

Father, in your teachings about divinity, you spoke in riddles and did not explain everything clearly. You said that no one can be saved without being reborn. When we climbed the mountain together, I asked you to teach me more about this rebirth, as it is the only thing I do not fully understand. You told me that I would learn it when I separated myself from the world. I have prepared myself and freed my mind from the distractions of the world.

Now, fulfill what you promised. Teach me about rebirth, whether openly or secretly. I don't know what substance or seed brings about this new birth, nor what kind of womb it comes from.

This knowledge, my son, must be understood in silence. The true Good is the seed of this rebirth.

But who plants this seed, Father? I am still confused and uncertain.

The seed is sown by the will of God, my son.

What kind of man is born through this process? I still cannot fully grasp it.

The one who is reborn becomes a child of God, a new person with divine understanding. God created the universe, filling it with all kinds of powers.

Father, you speak in riddles again and not plainly, as a father should speak to his son.

Son, this is not something that can be taught directly. It is given by God when He wills it, and He helps us remember it.

You are speaking of things that seem too distant and impossible, Father. I must challenge what you are saying.

Will you deny your father's wisdom, my son?

Please forgive me, Father. I am your son by nature. Tell me clearly how rebirth happens.

There is nothing more I can say than this: I have experienced a vision, given to me through God's mercy. I have left behind my old self and entered into an immortal body. I am not who I was before, for I have been reborn in mind.

This truth cannot be taught or seen with physical eyes. I left behind the material world, stepping away from it. Though I once knew and touched it, I am now separated from it.

Even if you look at me with your eyes, you cannot understand what I have become. Your physical sight will not reveal it.

Father, you have confused me deeply. I no longer know what to think about myself.

I wish, my son, that you could leave yourself behind as in a dream, when the mind roams free during sleep.

Then tell me, Father, who brings about this rebirth?

It is the child of God, created through the will of God.

You have silenced me, Father. All my previous thoughts have vanished. I now see only the emptiness in the things of this world, as they constantly change and decay. What is real, Father?

What is real, my son, is that which is not troubled or confined, not colored or shaped, not changed by anything. It is pure, high, and unchanging, understood only by itself and without form.

You have made me feel lost, Father. I thought you were leading me to wisdom, but now I feel my mind slipping away.

Yet it is exactly as I have said, my son. Those who focus only on things that rise like fire, fall like earth, flow like water, or move like air, cannot grasp what has no shape, weight, or form. They cannot understand what can only be known through its power and action. I pray to the divine Mind to reveal to us the meaning of this rebirth.

Father, I don't think I can understand it.

God forbid, my son. You must seek Him, and He will come to you. Be willing, and it will happen. Quiet the senses of your body, and free yourself from the desires that trap you in the material world.

Do I really have these traps within me, Father?

Yes, my son, and there are many of them. Some are quite powerful.

I don't know them, Father. What are they?

Ignorance is one. Sorrow is another. There is also lack of self-control, desire, injustice, greed, deceit, envy, fraud, anger, recklessness, and malice. These twelve are just the beginning. Many others torment the soul through the body, forcing it to suffer deeply.

These forces do not leave easily, even from those who receive God's mercy. This is both the challenge and the purpose of rebirth.

So now, my son, stay silent and praise God in your heart. In silence, we open ourselves to God's mercy, which will never fail us.

Rejoice, my son, for you are now cleansed by the power of God and ready to know the truth.

The knowledge of God has been revealed to us, casting out all ignorance. With knowledge comes joy, and when joy arrives, sorrow is driven away from those who embrace it.

Let us welcome temperance, the sweet power that brings self-control. When temperance arrives, it casts out all excess and restores balance.

Next, we embrace self-discipline, which gives us control over our desires. This, my son, is the firm foundation of justice.

See how, without effort, self-discipline has driven away injustice. When injustice is gone, we are made just.

Then comes the power of generosity, which removes greed from within us.

And when greed is gone, we welcome truth. With truth, all falsehood and deceit vanish.

See, my son, how the Good is made complete by the arrival of Truth. With Truth comes the end of envy, for Truth always brings the Good, along with Life and Light. Darkness and its torments disappear, fleeing suddenly and in confusion, unable to remain.

You now understand the process of rebirth, for when these ten powers arrive, the intellectual rebirth is complete. These powers drive away the twelve torments, as we have witnessed in the process of this transformation. Whoever receives this rebirth through God's mercy leaves behind all physical senses and realizes that they are made of divine things. Such a person rejoices, becoming stable and unchanging through God's work.

I understand now, Father, not with my physical eyes, but through the power of the mind. I feel present in heaven, on earth, in water, in air, in living beings, in plants, and in the womb—everywhere.

Please tell me one more thing. How do the twelve torments of darkness get expelled by the ten powers? How does this work, Trismegistus?

This body, my son, is like the circle of the zodiac, made up of twelve parts but also connected as one whole. All of nature uses different combinations to mislead humans. Although these forces seem separate, they act together. For example, anger always follows rashness. These forces are chaotic, and that is why they are driven away by the ten powers—powers that align with the dead.

The number ten, my son, is the giver of souls. It is where Life and Light unite, and from this unity, the spirit brings forth the power of oneness. In this way, the number ten represents unity, and unity contains the number ten.

Now I see both the universe and myself clearly within the mind, Father.

This is what rebirth means, my son: that we no longer fix our thoughts on the physical body, which exists in three dimensions. As we have discussed, we must not misjudge the universe by focusing only on the material.

Tell me, Father, will this body made of powers ever dissolve?

Speak carefully, my son, and do not entertain impossible thoughts. Doing so leads the mind away from truth and into error.

The physical body, being part of nature, is subject to decay. But the spiritual generation is not—it is beyond decay and immortal. Do you not understand that you are born a god, a child of the One, just as I am?

Father, I wish I could hear that hymn of praise you mentioned, the one you heard from the Powers when I was still within the Octonary.

As Pimander revealed to the Octonary, "You are right to seek the dissolution of the physical body, for you have been purified." Pimander, the mind of supreme authority, has shared only what is written, knowing that I can understand and perceive everything on my own. He commanded me to act only in ways that are good, and so the powers within me sing in harmony.

I wish to hear this song and understand it, Father.

Be still, my son, and listen closely to the hymn of thanksgiving—the hymn of rebirth. I had not intended to speak of it so clearly, but I will reveal it to you now, at the end of everything.

This teaching is not something that can be spoken openly; it must be kept in silence.

So now, my son, stand in the open air. Offer your worship while facing the north wind as the sun sets, and turn toward the south when the sun rises. Now, remain silent.

THE SECRET SONG. The Holy Speech.

Let all of nature listen to this hymn. Open up, O Earth, and release all the treasures of the rain. Trees, do not tremble, for I will sing and praise the Lord, the Creator of all things, the One who is everything. Open, O Heavens, and you Winds, be still, so the eternal circle of God may receive these words. I will sing and praise the One who created everything, who set the earth in place, who hung the heavens above, and commanded the sweet waters of the ocean to flow throughout the world, to nourish both inhabited and uninhabited lands, providing for all things and all people.

He gave fire to shine for every purpose, to serve both gods and men. Let us all give blessing to the One who rides through the heavens, the Creator of all nature. He is the eye of the mind, and He accepts the praises from within me. All the powers within me, praise the One and the All. Join with my will, all you powers within me, and sing with me. O holy knowledge, through your light I magnify the divine light, rejoicing in the joy of the mind.

Sing with me, all the powers that dwell within me. Now, my self-discipline, praise with me. Righteousness, sing with me and celebrate what is just. O spirit of communion within me, offer praise

44

to the All. Through me, truth gives praise to truth, and the good praises the good. O Life and Light, we offer this praise and thanksgiving to you. I thank you, O Father, for the work of the powers within me. I thank you, O God, for being the source of all my actions. Through me, the Word sings praise to you. Receive this offering of words as a reasonable sacrifice.

The powers within me cry out these praises, fulfilling your will. Your will flows from you and returns to you. O All, receive this offering of reason from everything that exists. O Life, save all that is within us. O Light, shine upon us. O God, guide the spirit, for the mind sustains the Word. O Spirit-bearing Creator, you are God. Through fire, air, earth, water, and spirit, your creation calls out to you.

From the beginning, I have found ways to bless and praise you, and I have gained what I sought—for I rest in your will.

Father, I see that you have sung this hymn with all your heart, and I have taken it into my world.

Speak of your inner world, my son.

Yes, Father, I mean my inner world. Through your hymn and words of praise, my mind has been filled with light. I wish to send my own thanks and praise to God from my understanding.

Do so carefully, my son.

It will come from my mind, Father.

The things I have seen and contemplated, I have shared with you. Now, my son Tat, the source of future generations, send these offerings of reason to God.

O God, you are the Father, the Lord, and the Mind. Accept these offerings of reason, which you have asked of me. All things happen according to your will, O Mind. My son, offer this pleasing sacrifice to God, the Father of all. Speak these words aloud as well.

Thank you, Father, for teaching me how to offer thanks and praise.

I am pleased, my son, to see truth bear the fruits of good things and immortal blessings. Learn this lesson from me: above all virtues, treasure silence. Do not share the sacred knowledge of rebirth with others, lest we be misunderstood or criticized. We have reflected enough—you through listening and I through speaking. Now you know yourself and our Father through the mind.

The Eighth Book,
The Greatest Evil in Man Is the Not Knowing God

Where are you headed, O men, drunk from the strong wine of ignorance? If you cannot bear it, why do you keep indulging and spilling it out again?

Stop, clear your minds, and lift your gaze with the eyes of your heart. And if not all of you can do this, let at least those who are able make the effort.

Ignorance surrounds the whole world like a poison, corrupting the soul trapped within the body, keeping it from reaching the harbor of salvation.

Don't let yourselves be swept along by the great current. Resist it if you can, and head toward the harbor of safety, steering your course directly toward it.

Search for someone who can take you by the hand and guide you to the doorway of truth and knowledge, where pure light shines without any darkness, where no one is drunk but all are sober and lift their hearts toward the One who desires to be known.

He cannot be heard with ears, nor seen with eyes, nor described with words, but only understood with the mind and heart.

First, you must tear apart the garment you wear—the web of ignorance that binds you. It is the source of all evil, the chain of corruption, the dark covering over your soul, a kind of living death. It is a burden you carry everywhere, a thief in your own home, pretending to love you but truly hating and envying you.

This harmful garment weighs you down, pulling you downward to keep you from looking upward and seeing the beauty of truth and the good that rests within it. If you saw it, you would despise the wickedness of this garment and recognize the traps it has set for you.

This garment works hard to make things that seem real feel pleasing to your senses. It hides what is truly real by covering it with distractions and burdens, filling your mind with harmful pleasures. As a result, you cannot hear what you need to hear or see what you need to see.

The Ninth Book,
A Universal Sermon to Asclepius

Everything that moves, Asclepius, must move in something and be moved by something, correct?

Yes, that's true.

Doesn't the space where something moves need to be larger than the thing that is moving within it?

Yes, it must be.

And isn't the force that moves something stronger than the thing being moved?

Yes, it is.

Then wouldn't the space in which something moves have to be opposite in nature to the thing being moved?

Yes, it must be.

Now, isn't this vast world a body, and isn't it the greatest of all bodies?

Yes, it is.

And isn't it solid, filled with many great bodies and, in fact, with all bodies that exist?

That's true.

The world is a body, and it moves, right?

Yes, it does.

Then what kind of space can hold something as large as the world and allow it to move freely? It must be far larger, so the world has room to move without being stopped or hindered, right?

Yes, it must be immense. But what kind of space would that be?

It must be something opposite in nature to a body, Asclepius. And isn't the nature of the non-physical opposite to that of the physical?

Yes, it is.

So, the space must be non-physical, and what is non-physical is either divine or God Himself. But by divine, I don't mean something created or born.

If it is divine, it is a kind of essence or being. But if it is God, it is something beyond essence, though it can be understood in a certain way.

God can be understood not by Himself but by us, because anything that can be understood is connected to a mind that perceives it.

Therefore, God does not understand Himself, since He is not separate from what He knows. But we are separate from Him, so we can understand Him.

If this space can be understood, then it is not just space—it is God. But if we understand God, we understand not a place but the way He acts and operates.

Everything that moves does so in something stable, not in another moving thing. And the force that causes movement remains stable while it moves other things, for it cannot move along with them.

But how is it, Trismegistus, that things here on Earth move along with other moving things? Didn't you say the wandering stars are moved by a fixed sphere?

That's not exactly what I meant, Asclepius. The wandering stars and the fixed sphere don't move together but in opposition to one another. They move in opposite ways, and that opposition creates a kind of balance, where movement is stabilized by resistance.

For example, the Bear constellation neither rises nor sets but keeps circling in place. Do you think it moves or stays still?

I think it moves, Trismegistus.

What kind of movement do you think it has?

It moves in a circular path, always revolving around the same point.

Exactly. The circular movement appears as though it's standing still because it moves in a way that keeps it bound to the same path. The opposition of these movements creates stability, keeping everything in place.

Let me give you a simple example from Earth. Consider a man swimming. As the water flows one way, he pushes against it with his hands and feet, holding his position. This resistance keeps him from being carried away or sinking beneath the water.

That's a very clear example, Trismegistus.

So, every movement depends on something stable and is guided by that stability.

The motion of the world and all material things does not come from outside the world but from within it, through a soul, a spirit, or some other non-physical force.

A lifeless body cannot move itself, nor can anything that is entirely lifeless.

But what do you mean, Trismegistus? Don't things like wood, stones, and other inanimate objects move too?

No, Asclepius, not on their own. Something within them causes movement. It's not the body itself that moves, but something alive within it that moves both the object carrying it and the object being

51

carried. One lifeless thing cannot move another—only something alive can cause movement.

Do you see now how the soul is burdened when it carries two bodies?

Yes, and it's clear now that everything that moves must move within and be moved by something.

Doesn't this mean, Trismegistus, that things moving in this world must be moving through empty space?

Be careful, Asclepius. Nothing that exists is truly empty. Only what does not exist can be called empty, for it is entirely outside of existence.

What exists must be full of being, for something that exists cannot be empty.

But aren't some things empty, Trismegistus, like an empty barrel, an empty jug, or an empty wine press?

Oh, Asclepius, you are mistaken. These things, which you believe to be empty, are actually full.

What do you mean, Trismegistus?

Isn't air a kind of body?

Yes, it is.

Then doesn't this body, air, pass through everything and fill everything it touches? And isn't air made up of a mixture of the four elements? So, all the things you call empty are actually full of air.

Instead of calling them empty, you should call them hollow, because they exist and are filled with air and spirit.

That makes perfect sense, Trismegistus. But what should we call the space where the entire universe moves?

Call it incorporeal, Asclepius.

What does that mean—incorporeal or without a body?

It refers to the mind and reason, which encompass everything and exist without a physical form. It cannot be touched or seen, and it is unaffected by anything physical. It is self-sufficient, capable of everything, and is the essence behind all things.

From it come goodness, truth, the original light, and the essence of the soul, like rays from the sun.

Then what is God?

God is none of these things directly, yet He is the source of them all. He is the cause of everything that exists, leaving nothing without being.

Everything that exists comes from things that already are, not from things that are not, because something that doesn't exist cannot produce anything. And what already exists cannot simply stop existing.

So, what exactly is God?

God is not just a mind, but the cause of mind. He is not just a spirit, but the cause of spirit. He is not light, but the cause of light.

Therefore, we must honor God with the two names that belong to Him alone: the Good and the Father.

He is nothing else beyond these names. Everything else is separate from the nature of goodness.

Neither the body nor the soul can contain true goodness.

The greatness of the Good is as vast as the existence of all things, both physical and non-physical, both visible and invisible.

This is the Good—God Himself.

Be careful never to call anything else good, for that would be disrespectful. And never call anyone else God, for only the Good is God.

Many people speak the word "good," but most do not understand what it truly means. Out of ignorance, they call gods and even people "good," though neither can ever truly be so.

The other gods are honored with the title of "god," but God is known as the Good—not by status in the heavens but by His very nature.

There is only one nature of God, and that is the Good. All kinds of beings come from this one source.

The one who is good gives everything and takes nothing. This is why God gives all things freely without ever receiving.

The other title we give Him is the Father, for it is the role of a father to create and give life.

That is why it has always been important for wise and virtuous people to have children.

On the other hand, to remain childless is seen as a misfortune and a wrongdoing. Those who die without children are punished by the spirits, for their souls are condemned to enter bodies that are neither male nor female—a cursed existence beneath the sun.

So, Asclepius, never celebrate a man's childlessness. Instead, pity him, knowing the punishment that awaits him after death.

Let this be a glimpse into the deeper truths of nature.

The Tenth Book,
The Mind to Hermes

Hold your speech, Hermes, and reflect on what has been said. But I will speak what is on my mind, for many people have shared different ideas about the universe and goodness, yet I have not discovered the truth.

May the Lord reveal the truth to me now, for I will trust only your explanation of these matters.

Then the Mind spoke of how everything is connected.

God and all things exist together.

God, Eternity, the World, Time, and Generation.

God created Eternity, Eternity created the World, the World brought forth Time, and Time brought about Generation.

From God comes goodness, beauty, blessedness, and wisdom.

From Eternity comes identity and consistency.

From the World comes order.

From Time comes change.

From Generation come life and death.

The workings of God are Mind and Soul.

Eternity brings permanence and immortality.

The World undergoes restoration and decay.

Time brings growth and decline.

Generation gives rise to different qualities.

Eternity belongs to God.

The World exists within Eternity.

Time operates within the World.

Generation unfolds within Time.

Eternity surrounds God.

The World moves within Eternity.

Time unfolds within the World.

Generation occurs within Time.

Therefore, God is the source of all things.

Eternity is the substance behind everything.

The World is the material that holds all things.

Eternity is the power of God.

The World, although ever-changing, is continuously created through the timeless nature of Eternity.

Nothing will ever be destroyed because Eternity is incorruptible.

Nor can anything perish within the World, as it is embraced by the eternal.

The wisdom of God consists of goodness, beauty, blessedness, virtue, and eternity.

Eternity grants matter immortality and everlasting nature, as Generation relies on Eternity just as Eternity relies on God.

Generation and Time operate in both Heaven and on Earth, but their nature differs: in Heaven, they are unchanging and incorruptible, while on Earth, they are subject to change and decay.

God is the soul of Eternity. Eternity is the soul of the World. Heaven is the soul of the Earth.

God resides within the Mind, the Mind within the Soul, and the Soul within matter—all sustained through Eternity.

The entire universe, and everything within it, is filled with soul. The soul holds the Mind, and the Mind is filled with God.

God fills everything from within and holds all things from without, giving life to the universe.

Externally, God gives life to the world, and internally, He breathes life into all living things.

Above, in Heaven, He remains constant and unchanging, while below on Earth, He governs the cycles of birth and transformation.

Eternity encompasses the World, whether through necessity, divine guidance, or natural law.

If anyone thinks otherwise, they misunderstand, for God governs everything.

God's power surpasses all, and nothing can compare, whether human or divine.

Do not mistake anything on Earth or in Heaven as being like God, for such a comparison would be false.

Nothing can resemble the One who is unlike anything else, nor has God shared His power with anything else.

Who else could create life, immortality, or transformation? And what else would God need to make?

God is not idle; if He were, everything would cease to be, for everything is sustained by Him.

There is no idleness anywhere in the universe, for nothing is empty of purpose—both the doer and the deed must exist.

All things must continue according to the nature of each place and being.

The One who creates is present in all things, yet He is not confined by anything. He does not focus on just one task but creates everything.

As the source of action and power, He sustains everything that exists, both beneath Him and under His command.

Look through my eyes, and you will see the world clearly and understand its beauty.

The world is a body that endures forever. Though ancient, it remains youthful and full of life.

Observe the seven heavenly realms above us, each following its own unchanging course, filling eternity with endless movement.

Everything is filled with light, yet fire is not found within it.

The harmonious blending of opposites creates light, through the operation of God, the source of all good, order, and harmony in the seven realms.

Look also upon the Moon, which leads the other heavenly bodies. It serves as an instrument of nature, guiding the transformations of matter here on Earth.

Behold the Earth at the center of all things, serving as the stable foundation of the world, nourishing and sustaining all earthly creatures.

Think about how many immortal and mortal beings exist, and notice how the Moon moves between both realms, touching both mortal and immortal things.

Everything is full of soul, and it is the soul that moves all things. Some things move around the heavens, and others move on the Earth. Yet none of them switch places—what is on the right does not go to the left, nor do things above descend downward, or things below rise upward.

You already know, Hermes, that all these things are created.

They are bodies with souls, and because they have souls, they are in motion.

But for all things to come together in unity, something must hold them together.

There must be a single force that brings everything into one.

Since the motions are so different, and the bodies are not alike, but still follow one orderly flow, it's clear that there cannot be more than one creator.

One creator alone ensures harmony in this order.

If there were many creators, they would envy each other, and that would lead to conflict.

If one creator made mortal beings, he would want to create immortal beings as well. Similarly, the creator of immortal beings would seek to make mortal ones.

And if there were two creators, which one would take charge of the future?

If both shared the responsibility, who would hold the greater power?

Every living being consists of both matter and soul, and is made of both mortal and immortal parts.

All living things have souls. The things that are lifeless are just raw matter.

The soul, as it draws closer to its creator, brings life and existence to everything. And because it is tied to life, it becomes the cause of immortality as well.

So what makes mortal beings different from immortal ones?

If the soul can create life and immortality, how could it not also create living beings?

It is clear that something is behind all of this, and it is just as clear that this force is one.

There is one soul, one life, and one matter.

And who else could this be but the One God?

Who else would have any reason to create life but God alone?

Therefore, there is only one God.

It would be absurd to say there is one world, one Sun, one Moon, and one divine order, yet believe in many gods.

This one God works through many things.

If you yourself are capable of doing many things—seeing, speaking, hearing, smelling, tasting, touching, walking, understanding, and breathing—why would it be difficult for God to create life, soul, immortality, and change?

It is not as though one part of you sees, another part hears, another speaks, and so on. It is one being—yourself—who does all these things.

In the same way, God is behind everything, for nothing can happen without Him.

Just as you would no longer be alive if you stopped doing all these things, God would not be God if He stopped creating.

And since nothing in the universe can remain idle or empty, how much more is this true for God?

If there were anything He could not do, it would mean He was imperfect, which is impossible.

Since God is perfect and never idle, He does everything.

Now listen carefully, Hermes. You will see that it is necessary for God to create everything that exists, has existed, or will exist.

This, my dear friend, is life.

This is beauty.

This is goodness.

This is God.

If you want to understand this through your own actions, think about what happens when you create something.

However, God is not driven by pleasure, nor does He have anyone else working alongside Him.

Being the sole creator, God is always working, and what He makes is part of Himself.

If anything were separated from Him, it would cease to exist, for nothing can live apart from Him.

Since all things in Heaven and on Earth are alive through Him, and since one life flows through all, everything is made by God.

Life is the union of mind and soul.

Death is not the destruction of what has been united, but the separation of their union.

The image of God is Eternity. The image of Eternity is the World. The image of the World is the Sun. And the image of the Sun is humanity.

People say that change is death because the body dissolves, and life returns to what is unseen.

But I tell you, Hermes, the world only changes; it does not dissolve. Each day, part of it becomes invisible, but it is never lost.

These are the transformations of the world—revolutions and hidden cycles. A revolution is a turning, and what is hidden is renewed.

The world is not shaped by things outside it but constantly changes within itself.

If the world is filled with forms, then what must its creator be like? The creator cannot be without form.

And if the creator is filled with every form, He will remain in harmony with the world. But if He had only one form, He would exist apart from the world and its cycles.

We must be careful not to question God with words, for we cannot know anything about Him with doubt in our minds.

God has a single idea, unique to Him. Because this idea is not physical, it cannot be seen, though it reveals itself through all physical forms.

Do not be surprised that such an incorruptible idea exists.

It is like the margins of written words. They may seem to rise and stand out, but in reality, they are smooth and level.

Understand this truth clearly: just as man cannot live without life, God cannot exist without doing good.

Doing good is the life and movement of God. He brings everything into motion and gives life to all.

Some of what I have said needs further explanation, so pay close attention.

Everything exists within God, but not as if placed in a physical space. Space is both physical and unchanging, while things that occupy space cannot move.

What lies within the unbodily is not the same as what appears to be in the physical world.

God contains everything, and nothing is greater, swifter, or stronger than what is not bound by a physical body. The unbodily is limitless in capacity, speed, and power.

To understand this, command your soul to go to a far-off place, like India. It will arrive there even faster than you can speak the command.

Tell it to cross the ocean, and it will instantly be there—not by traveling, but by simply being there.

Command your soul to fly into the heavens, and it will rise without wings. Nothing can stop it—not the heat of the sun, not the ether, not the movements of the stars. It will pass through everything and reach the furthest heights.

If you wish to see what lies beyond the universe, you can.

This is the power and speed your soul holds. If you can do such things, how could God not do the same?

Now, think of God as holding the entire universe within His mind, as if it were all thoughts or ideas.

To understand God, you must become like Him.

Only something like God can understand God.

You must expand yourself beyond all limits—beyond the physical body, beyond time itself. Become one with eternity, and only then will you grasp the nature of God.

Believe that nothing is impossible for you. Consider yourself immortal, capable of understanding everything—every art, every science, and every way of life.

Imagine yourself as greater than the highest heights and deeper than the lowest depths. Contain within yourself the qualities of all things: fire, water, dryness, moisture. Be everywhere at once—in the sea, on the earth.

Understand yourself as unborn, young, old, alive, and dead, all at the same time. Know everything about time, places, actions, qualities, and amounts. Only by doing so will you begin to understand God.

But if you lock your soul within your body and misuse it, saying, "I understand nothing. I can do nothing. I am afraid of the sea. I cannot reach the heavens. I don't know who I am. I don't know what I will become," then you have no connection to God.

You will not be able to understand the beauty and goodness of God. Instead, you will be tied to the desires of the body and all that is evil.

The greatest evil is not knowing God.

But the path to knowing Him is simple: you must desire to know, hope to understand, and believe in your ability to do so. This is the divine way, the way of goodness.

This path will appear to you everywhere—when you are awake or asleep, sailing or traveling, speaking or silent, by day or night.

For everything reflects the image of God.

Though you say that God is invisible, nothing is clearer than Him.

He made all things so that you could see Him in everything.

This is God's goodness and power—to make Himself known and visible in all things.

Even what is not physical can still be seen.

The mind is seen through understanding, and God is seen through creation and action.

Let this be clear to you, Hermes.

Apply this same way of thinking to everything, and you will not go astray.

The Eleventh Book
The Common Mind, To Tat

The Mind, Tat, is part of God's essence, if God has any essence that we can know. Only God knows exactly what that essence is. The Mind is not separate from God's essence but connected to it, like the light from the sun. In humans, this Mind is God, which makes some humans nearly divine, with their humanity closely connected to divinity. The good spirit even called the gods "immortal men" and referred to men as "mortal gods."

In animals, which lack reason, the Mind works as their natural instinct. Where there is a soul, there is a mind, just as where there is life, there is a soul. In creatures without reason, the soul provides life but lacks the operations of the Mind. In humans, however, the Mind guides the soul toward goodness. In animals, it cooperates with their instincts, but in humans, it works against their lower desires.

Once the soul enters the body, it becomes corrupted by sorrow, pain, and pleasure. These emotions flow from the physical body, and the soul is stained by them, like a sponge absorbing liquid. But when the Mind leads the soul, it offers its light, resisting the soul's tendencies toward pleasure and false beliefs. Just as a skilled doctor may hurt the body to heal it by cutting or burning away disease, the Mind causes discomfort to the soul by pulling it away from pleasure, the source of spiritual sickness. The greatest sickness of the soul is denying God, which leads to all other evils and blocks all good.

The Mind helps the soul, just as a physician heals the body. But those souls that reject the guidance of the Mind are left to follow their desires, much like animals. These people give in to every craving, moving toward a life like that of beasts. They act with anger and desire without reason, never satisfied and always trapped in their impulses. Uncontrolled anger and unchecked desires are among the worst evils.

To prevent this, God placed the Mind within humans as a judge, to correct and restrain them.

You mentioned earlier, Tat, that fate determines our actions, so what happens when someone does evil like adultery or theft? If these actions are determined by fate, how can the person be held responsible and punished? Isn't that unjust?

Everything, Tat, happens according to fate. Nothing, good or bad, happens without it. But it is also part of fate that those who commit evil must suffer the consequences of their actions. They are destined to experience the results of what they do, and they do wrong so that they may endure punishment. Let's leave this discussion about fate and evil for now, though, as we've explored it before.

Right now, we are discussing the Mind and its role. In animals, the Mind works through instinct, but in humans, it restrains both anger and desire. Some humans follow reason, while others do not. But all are subject to fate, change, and the cycle of birth and death. These are the boundaries set by fate. Everyone must experience what fate has decreed.

However, those guided by the Mind experience these things differently. Although they may suffer the same external troubles, they do not suffer in the same way as those who are ruled by anger and desire.

What do you mean, Father? Isn't someone who commits adultery or murder an evil person?

The one ruled by the Mind, my son, does not suffer punishment as the adulterer or murderer does. They may face the consequences of actions, but not because they are consumed by evil themselves.

Change is unavoidable, but those with the Mind's guidance can escape the grip of vice.

I once heard the good spirit say, though he did not write it down, that everything is connected as one, especially things understood by the Mind. All that exists is part of one reality. We exist in action, power, and eternity.

A good soul is one with the Mind, and when the soul is united with the Mind, it is connected to all things. Therefore, all things known through the Mind are united. Just as the Mind governs everything, the soul that comes from God can do whatever it wills.

This answers the question you asked earlier about the connection between fate and the Mind. If you withdraw from arguments and distractions, you will see that the soul connected to the Mind is above fate and the laws that bind ordinary things. Nothing is impossible for the Mind, not even what fate controls.

Even though the soul is above fate, it should still pay attention to the things governed by fate. This, Tat, is what the good spirit taught.

Father, your words are insightful and profound, but I still need clarity on one thing. You said that in animals, the Mind follows their natural instincts. But if the Mind cooperates with these instincts, which are driven by emotions and desires, does that mean the Mind itself becomes emotional and driven by passions?

That's an excellent question, my son. And you are right to ask it. Let me explain.

All non-physical things that exist in the body are subject to emotions, and in a way, they are emotions themselves. Everything that causes movement is non-physical, while everything that is moved is physical. The Mind causes movement, and through movement, both the mover and the thing being moved experience emotion. Even rulers and those they rule experience emotions through this movement. When the soul is freed from the body, it is also freed from these emotions.

In truth, nothing in existence is completely free from emotion; everything is affected by it in some way. But there is a difference between emotion itself and the thing that experiences it. Emotions cause actions, while those affected by emotions experience them. Physical bodies act in one way or another—they either stay still or move—and both states are forms of emotional experience. Non-physical things, on the other hand, are always active, and because of this, they too experience emotion.

Don't let these words confuse you, though. Action and emotion are closely connected, but it is more respectful to use the word "action."

Consider this as well: God has given humanity two great gifts—Mind and Reason. These gifts are so powerful that they are equal to immortality. If someone uses these gifts correctly, they will be no different from the gods. When they leave their physical body, these gifts will guide them to join the divine beings.

Do other living creatures have speech, Father?

No, my son. They only have voice. There is a big difference between speech and voice. Speech belongs to all of humanity, while voice belongs to individual creatures according to their kind.

But Father, people speak differently in different countries.

That is true, but just as all people are part of humanity, speech is still one. It may sound different in Egypt, Persia, or Greece, but its essence remains the same everywhere. You seem to underestimate the power and importance of speech, my son. The good spirit once revealed that the soul belongs in the body, the mind in the soul, and speech in the mind, with God as the source of all.

Speech is the expression of the mind, just as the mind reflects God. The body is the form of an idea, and the idea flows from the soul. The most subtle part of matter is air, from which the soul emerges. From the soul comes the mind, and from the mind comes God.

God is present in everything and through everything. The mind governs the soul, the soul controls the air, and the air surrounds matter. Meanwhile, destiny, providence, and nature are tools that shape the material world.

All non-physical things share the same essence, which is identity. But physical things are made up of many parts that change, even though their underlying identity remains the same. In every physical object, there is a certain number, and without numbers, nothing can be built, combined, or dissolved. Numbers are born from unity, and when they dissolve, they return to unity.

All things are united by matter. This entire world is like a great god, connected to a higher one, and it is filled with life through the will of the Father. Nothing in the world, whether as a whole or in its parts, is without life. There is nothing dead in the world— nothing that was, is, or will be. The Father wants the world to be alive for as long as it exists, and because of that, it must also be divine.

How can anything be dead in a universe that reflects God and is filled with life? Death is decay, and decay is destruction. But nothing in an incorruptible world can decay, and nothing connected to God can be destroyed.

But don't living things in the world die, Father?

Be careful with your words, my son. What you call "death" is just the dissolving of physical forms. Dissolution is not the same as destruction. Things are not dissolved to disappear but to be made new.

What, then, is life? Isn't it movement?

Yes, and everything in the world is in motion, my son.

But Father, doesn't the Earth seem still?

No, my son. It moves in many ways, even though it may seem stable. It would be strange if the Earth, which gives life to all things, did not move. Nothing can create life without movement. It is absurd to think that any part of the universe could be inactive, for inactivity means nothingness.

Everything in the world moves either by growing or by diminishing. Whatever moves also has life, but life does not need to stay the same. While the universe as a whole remains unchanged, its parts are always changing. Yet nothing is ever truly destroyed. What troubles people is not reality but the names they use for things.

Creation is not the same as life; it is the process of making things visible. Likewise, change is not death; it is the hiding of what once was. All things—matter, life, spirit, soul, and mind—are immortal. Every living thing is immortal because of the mind within it, but especially humans, who receive God and communicate with Him.

God speaks to people in many ways—through dreams at night and through signs during the day. He also gives messages through birds, the wind, and even trees.

Humans have the unique ability to understand what has happened in the past, what is happening now, and what will happen in the future. Think also, my son, about how other creatures only live in specific parts of the world. Fish live in water, land animals on the earth, and birds in the air. But humans interact with all elements—earth, water, air, and even fire—and they experience the heavens through their senses.

God, however, exists everywhere and in everything. He is both action and power. Understanding God is not as difficult as it may seem. If you wish to see him, look at the necessity in all things around you and the way events unfold with purpose. Notice how life fills the material world and how God moves everything—bringing good into gods, spirits, and people alike.

If these things are indeed actions, as you've said, then they are performed by none other than God. Just as the world has its different parts—heaven, earth, water, and air—God has his aspects, which include life, immortality, eternity, spirit, necessity, providence, nature, soul, and mind. All of these parts remain constant and are part of what we call the Good.

There is no place, no moment, and no thing—past or present—where God is absent.

What about matter, Father? Does God exist in matter as well?

How could matter exist without God? If you imagine matter as an inactive pile of material, you misunderstand its nature. If it is active, then it must be God who gives it motion. We've already said that actions are the parts of God. So, who brings life to living things? Who grants immortality to the eternal? Who causes things to change? All of these processes come from God.

Whether we speak of matter, body, or essence, we are talking about acts of God. Matter behaves as matter because of God. Bodies exist as physical things through his power, and essence becomes what it is through him. God is present in everything. There is nothing within creation that is not part of God.

This means that we cannot think of God in terms of size, place, shape, or even time. He is all things, present in all things, and beyond all things. Worship this truth, my son. The only way to truly serve God is to live without doing evil.

The Twelfth Book, His Crater or Monas

The Creator made the universe, not with hands, but through His Word. Think of Him as always present everywhere, creating everything by His will. His body is not something you can touch, see, measure, or contain. It isn't fire, water, air, or wind, though all these come from Him. Being the ultimate Good, He has taken that name for Himself alone.

He also adorned the Earth with divine beauty and sent humanity into the world—both immortal and mortal beings at once. Humans are above other creatures and the rest of creation because they have both speech and mind. Humans witness the works of God, marvel at them, and recognize Him as the Creator.

While God gave speech to all people, He did not give mind to everyone. Yet, He did not withhold it out of envy, for envy does not reach Him. It exists only in the hearts of people without the gift of mind.

Why, Father, didn't God give mind to everyone?

Because it pleased Him to place it in the center of all souls as a reward to be earned.

Where did He place it?

He filled a great cup with mind and sent it down, along with a messenger to make an announcement.

The messenger proclaimed to all souls: "Come, all who are able, and immerse yourselves in this cup. Those who believe they will return to the One who sent this cup, and those who know their true purpose, come and take part."

Those who understood the message and immersed themselves in the mind became enlightened and perfect, sharing in knowledge. But those who missed the call received only speech, not mind. They do not know why they were created or by whom. Their senses make them like animals, filled with anger and desires. They do not admire what is worthy of awe but chase after bodily pleasures, thinking that life was made only for these things.

However, those who receive God's gift are more like immortals than mortals. They understand all things on Earth, in the heavens, and even beyond. Rising above the world, they see the Good and recognize that staying here is a burden. They despise all things, both material and immaterial, and seek only the One.

This is what it means to know the mind—seeing the divine and understanding God. The cup filled with mind is itself divine.

And I, Father, wish to be immersed in that cup.

You cannot love yourself, my son, until you first reject your attachment to the body. Only by loving yourself will you receive the mind, and only by receiving the mind will you gain true knowledge.

What do you mean, Father?

You cannot focus on both mortal and divine things at the same time. Mortal things are tied to the body, while divine things are not. You must choose between the two, for no one can have both. Whichever you choose will grow stronger, while the other fades away.

Choosing the higher path brings out the best in a person and connects them with God. It shows reverence and devotion. But choosing the lower path leads to ruin, though it does not harm God. Those who follow the lower path are like performers in a show—they make a spectacle of themselves in the world, misled by bodily pleasures.

Since God has given us so much, let us also be generous, without holding back. God is pure and blameless; we are the ones who cause evil by choosing it over the Good.

See how many layers of existence we must pass through—how many spirits and stars we must rise above—to reach the One true God. The Good cannot be surpassed. It is infinite, without beginning or end, though it seems to begin for us when we first come to know it.

Our knowledge of the Good does not mark its true beginning, only the beginning of our awareness of it. Once we grasp that beginning, we can move quickly through all things.

It is difficult to turn away from the familiar things of this world and return to the ancient truths. The things we see attract us, making it hard to believe in what cannot be seen. The things most visible are often evil, while the Good remains hidden. The Good has no shape or form and resembles nothing else.

That is why the Good seems unlike everything else. An immaterial thing cannot be revealed to a physical body. This is the difference between things that are alike and those that are not. Things that are unlike always fall short of those that are alike.

The One is the root and source of all things. Nothing can exist without a beginning, but the Beginning itself has no origin—it exists by itself and is the foundation of everything else. Because it does not come from another, it simply is.

Unity is the beginning of all things, containing every number while being contained by none. It creates all numbers but is not created by any number.

Everything that is created or made is imperfect, meaning it can be divided, increased, or diminished. But what is truly perfect is not subject to any of these changes.

Whatever grows does so through unity, but if it lacks the strength to hold on to unity, it weakens, fades, and disappears.

This is the image of God that I have described to you as best as I can, Tat. If you carefully reflect on it with the eyes of your mind, you will find the path that leads to higher truths. In fact, the image itself will guide you toward them.

What is remarkable about this vision is that it draws those who are able to see it closer, holding them fast. It pulls them toward itself, just as a magnet attracts iron.

The Thirteenth Book,
Sense and Understanding

Yesterday, Asclepius, I shared a complete teaching, but today I feel it is important to also talk about sense.

Sense and understanding seem to be different because sense is tied to the physical world, while understanding belongs to the essence of things. However, I believe they are closely connected in human beings. In other creatures, sense works with their nature, but in people, it is linked with understanding.

The mind is different from understanding, just as divinity is distinct from God. Divinity flows from God, and understanding flows from the mind. Understanding and speech work together; neither can exist fully without the other. You can't express words without understanding, and understanding isn't revealed without words.

In humans, sense and understanding are closely intertwined. It's impossible to fully understand without sense, and you can't experience sense without understanding. However, the mind can understand without sense for a time, such as when we dream and experience visions.

I believe that both sense and understanding are active in dreams, awakening the mind. A person's body and soul work together, and when they are in harmony, the mind produces understanding. The mind gives birth to thoughts. Good thoughts come from seeds planted by God, while harmful thoughts arise from seeds sown by demons.

There is no part of the world untouched by evil. Evil spirits secretly plant harmful seeds in the mind, leading people toward actions like adultery, murder, disrespect for parents, and other destructive deeds. These actions come from the seeds of evil spirits.

In contrast, God's seeds are fewer, but they are great, beautiful, and good—virtue, self-control, and piety. Piety is the knowledge of God. Those who know God are filled with good things and possess divine understanding, setting them apart from most people.

Because they have this knowledge, they often do not fit in with the majority. They may be misunderstood, mocked, or even hated. Some are killed because their understanding clashes with the wickedness that prevails on earth.

Wickedness resides on earth, not in the higher realms, even though some may wrongly claim otherwise. A person who knows God will reject wickedness and rise above it. Even though certain things seem evil to others, those who know God see everything as good.

They reflect deeply and come to see everything through the lens of knowledge. Amazingly, they can even turn bad things into something good.

Now, let's return to the topic of sense. Humans are unique because they combine sense with understanding. However, not every person achieves understanding. Some people are dominated by material desires, while others pursue essential truths.

Those focused on material things receive their understanding from evil spirits. But those who seek the good are connected to God. God works through nature, making all things good, just like Himself.

Even though God makes things good, the way they are used in the world can become unlawful or harmful. The movement of the universe generates different qualities, some leading to evil and others to goodness.

The world has its own sense and understanding, different from that of humans. The world's understanding is simpler and more unified. It creates all things and takes them back into itself, following God's will. The world acts as a tool of God, receiving seeds from Him, bringing things into existence, and renewing them through dissolution.

The world is like a farmer of life. When things die or break apart, it sows new seeds, giving birth to new life. Everything in the world is alive, and life flows from the world's constant movement. The world is both the source and the sustainer of life.

The elements that form bodies—earth, water, air, and fire—combine in various ways. Some bodies are more complex, while others are simpler. Heavier bodies are made from more elements, while lighter ones are made from fewer.

The movement of the world influences the qualities of everything born within it. The flow of life touches all things, shaping their nature.

God is the father of the world, and the world is the father of all things within it. The world is God's child, and everything within the world is a child of the world.

That's why the world is called an "ornament"—because it beautifully decorates everything with the endless variety of life. Through constant motion and the blending of elements, the world brings everything to life. This is why it is fitting to call it the world, for it adorns creation with unceasing life and beauty.

All living beings receive both sense and understanding from the outside, through what surrounds and sustains them. The world, having once received these gifts from God when it was created, still holds them today.

But God is not, as some mistakenly think through superstition, without sense or understanding. Everything that exists is in God, made by Him, and depends on Him. Some things operate through their bodies, others move through a soul-like essence, some are energized by a spirit, while others receive rest—everything functioning as it should.

It is more accurate to say that God does not possess these things, but instead is all things. He does not take anything in from outside but instead expresses everything outwardly. This is God's way of knowing and understanding—constantly moving everything.

There will never be a time when anything that exists will stop or disappear. When I speak of "things that are," I mean God. For everything that exists is part of God, and nothing exists apart from Him, just as He exists in everything.

If you understand these ideas, Asclepius, you will find them true. But if you do not understand, they may seem unbelievable. To understand is to believe, and not believing means you do not understand. Words alone cannot reach the truth, but the mind, guided by speech for a time, can eventually grasp it.

When the mind recognizes how everything connects and aligns with the truths shared through speech, it rests in trust and belief. For those who understand these teachings about God, they are believable, but for those who do not, they remain beyond belief.

This is what I have to say about understanding and sense.

The Fourteenth Book
Operation and Sense

The ability to sense and understand comes to all living beings from the outside, through the influence of what surrounds and sustains them. The world, having once received this gift from God at creation, continues to carry it within.

Some people mistakenly believe that God has no sense or understanding, but this is a misunderstanding born of superstition. In truth, everything exists in God, is made by God, and depends on Him. Some things work through their bodies, others move with a soul-like force, and some operate by spirit—all fitting perfectly into their roles.

It is not that God simply possesses these things, but rather He is all these things. He does not gather them from the outside but expresses them outwardly. God's way of knowing is to be the constant force that moves everything.

There will never be a time when what exists ceases or disappears. When I speak of "the things that are," I refer to God, for everything exists within God, and nothing can exist apart from Him, nor is He separate from anything.

If you understand these truths, Asclepius, they will seem clear and true. But if you do not understand, they will seem unbelievable. To understand is to believe, and to lack belief means you have not yet understood. Words alone cannot reach the full truth, but the mind, when guided by speech, can find its way to it.

When the mind sees how everything aligns with the truths we have discussed, it finds peace in belief. To those who understand what has been said about God, these things will seem credible. But for those who do not understand, they will seem impossible to believe.

This, then, is my teaching on the nature of understanding and sense.

Without these elements, the body would not be able to function. Other operations are specific to human souls, expressed through arts, sciences, studies, and actions. These operations also give rise to the senses, or at least perfect them.

Understand, my son, that these operations come from a higher source. While the senses belong to the body and arise from it, they only manifest once an operation brings them to life, making them seem physical. This is why I say that the senses are both physical and mortal. They exist only as long as the body exists, since they are born with the body and die with it.

Mortal things, however, do not have senses because they lack the necessary essence. The senses can only grasp physical experiences of good or bad that affect the body. But external objects do not receive or lose anything in the same way, so they do not have senses.

Do the senses work in every body, you ask? Yes, they do, my son. And do operations act in all things? Yes, even in lifeless things, though the senses differ. In rational beings, the senses operate with reason. In irrational creatures, the senses are purely physical. In lifeless things, the senses only react passively through growth and decay.

Passion and sense are connected at a higher level, both coming together through operations. In living creatures, two more forces follow the senses and passions—grief and pleasure. Without these, no living being, especially one capable of reason, could experience or understand anything.

I call these the ruling ideas of passion, especially in rational beings. Operations carry out actions, but the senses reveal these actions. Since the senses are connected to the lower parts of the soul, they can cause harm. What brings pleasure often becomes the source of suffering for the one who indulges in it. And sorrow brings even stronger pain, showing that both pleasure and sorrow are harmful forces.

The same is true of the soul's own sense. But isn't the soul non-physical, while the senses belong to the body, you ask? Or do the senses exist within the body? If we say that the senses belong in the body, we might mistakenly compare them to the soul or to operations, since both of these are non-physical but act through bodies.

However, the senses are neither operations, nor part of the soul, nor part of the body itself. They exist as something in between, as we have said before. Because the senses are not non-physical, they must be considered physical. Everything that exists is either a body or something without a body.

The Fifteenth Book,
Truth to His Son Tat

Humans, being imperfect creatures made of many different parts, cannot speak about truth with complete confidence. True reality only exists in eternal things, where even their very nature is true. Fire is purely fire, earth is only earth, air is solely air, and water is entirely water. But our bodies are made of a mixture of all these elements, and because they are mixed, none of them can be fully true within us.

If our original nature didn't contain truth, how could we ever see, speak, or understand truth unless God allowed it? On Earth, what we see is not truth but only imitations of it, and even these are rare. Most things are filled with falsehood and deception, appearing only as images shaped by our imagination. When our imagination receives guidance from above, it can reflect some aspects of truth, but without that influence, it remains a lie.

An image may resemble the body it portrays, but it is not that body. It may have eyes but cannot see, and it may show ears but cannot hear. It deceives the viewer into believing they are seeing the real thing when in fact, it is just an illusion.

Those who do not recognize falsehood are able to see the truth. If we see things exactly as they are, we understand truth. But if we perceive them differently from what they are, we cannot grasp truth.

You ask if truth exists on Earth. The answer, my son, is no—truth cannot exist here because it cannot be created or made. However, some individuals, with God's guidance, might come to understand glimpses of it. To the mind and reason of men, nothing on Earth is truly real. Everything here is just an appearance, a fleeting image, or an opinion.

You ask whether speaking about things as they are can be called truth. But there is no real truth on Earth. You wonder how we can even claim to know that truth doesn't exist if nothing here is true. Understand this: truth is the most perfect virtue and the highest form of good. It is pure, unchangeable, and unaffected by the material world. It does not have a body and remains constant and clear.

The things here on Earth are always changing and decaying. They are temporary, corruptible, and full of imperfections. How can anything be true if it is always shifting and never remains the same? When something changes, it becomes a lie, showing us different forms instead of staying consistent.

You ask if humans can be considered true. As long as someone is human, they cannot be true. Truth belongs only to what stays unchanged and remains the same forever. Humans are made of many parts and do not remain the same. They change over time, both in appearance and in character, going through stages and transformations during their lives.

People may not even recognize their own children or parents after some time has passed. How can something so changeable be considered true? Instead, it is false, appearing in many different forms throughout life. True things stay constant and unchanging, but people are not constant, so they cannot be truly real. Humans are like fleeting images, and every appearance is ultimately a form of falsehood.

Even the eternal bodies in the universe, though they may seem constant, are not truly real because they too undergo change. Things that are created or altered cannot be fully true, although they might contain elements of truth since they come from the source of all creation. Yet, because they change, they also carry some degree of falsehood.

Something that cannot stay the same is not true. You ask if the sun is the only thing that can be called true because it seems unchanging. Yes, the sun is closer to truth because it stays constant and plays a vital role in shaping the world. It governs creation, maintaining the world's order. I honor and respect the truth that the sun represents, acknowledging it as the work of the Creator.

You wonder what the first and highest truth is. It is the One—without matter, without shape, without color or form, and unchanging. It always remains the same. Falsehood, on the other hand, is tied to corruption, and everything on Earth is affected by it.

Corruption is necessary for new things to be created. Everything that is born or created must eventually decay so that more can be generated. In this way, creation and decay are intertwined, ensuring that life continues without end.

Recognize the original Creator through the act of creation. The things that come into existence through corruption are not true because they are constantly changing—one thing becomes another. It is impossible for these things to remain the same, and if something is not the same, how can it be true?

Therefore, we must understand these things as mere appearances or illusions. If we wish to describe people accurately, we must say that what we see are appearances. A man is the appearance of a man, a child is the appearance of a child, an old man is the appearance of old age, a young man is the appearance of youth, and a person in their prime is the appearance of maturity.

A man is not truly a man, just as a child is not truly a child, nor is an old man truly old. The same is true for all other stages of life. These appearances change over time, which means they are not real. The things that existed before and the things that exist now are always shifting, and because of this, they are false.

Understand this, my son: these false appearances and changing forms still have their origin in the truth, which comes from above. Even though these shifting forms seem false, they still originate from the source of truth itself.

In this way, falsehood can be understood as a product of truth.

The Sixteenth Book,
That None of The Things That Can
Perish

We must now talk about the soul and the body, my son, and how the soul is immortal and what happens to the body when it forms and when it dissolves. But there is no such thing as death in any of these processes. Death is just a word, either meaningless or misunderstood, for it suggests an end to something that is truly immortal.

Death implies destruction, but nothing in the universe is ever really destroyed. If the world is like a second god, an immortal living being, then no part of something immortal can die. Everything in the world is connected to the whole, and this includes humans, who are rational beings.

God, who is eternal and uncreated, is the source of all things. The world is the second creation, formed in God's image. It is sustained, nurtured, and made eternal by God, who acts as its father, keeping it alive forever. The world is both immortal and ever-living.

There is a difference between being eternal and being ever-living. What is eternal has no beginning, and if it did have a beginning, it created itself without help from anything else. Eternity is always complete in itself. The eternal, then, is the entire universe.

God, the Father, is eternal on His own. The world was made by God and is always living and immortal. God took all the available matter and shaped it into a body, making it round like a sphere. He gave it qualities and infused it with immortality so that it would never fall into disorder.

The Father, filled with endless ideas, placed these qualities within the spheres, sealing them into circles. His intention was to bring beauty and order to everything that was to be created. He covered the whole universe with immortality so that the matter would not break apart into chaos if it tried to separate from its structure.

When matter was first formed into bodies, it existed in disorder. This same disorder continues to revolve through all material things, growing and shrinking in cycles, which people mistakenly call death. In truth, it is simply disorder occurring within earthly beings.

The heavenly bodies follow a fixed order given to them by the Father, one that remains unchanging and eternal. Earthly bodies, however, undergo change. When they dissolve, they return to their pure, undivided state, becoming immortal once again. This process causes them to lose their senses temporarily, but it does not destroy the body.

The third type of living being is man, created in the image of the world. By the Father's will, humans possess a higher mind than other earthly creatures. Humans are connected to the second god, which is the world, and they also have the capacity to understand the first god, who is beyond all form.

Humans comprehend the second god, the world, through the body, but they understand the first god as something incorporeal— the pure mind of goodness.

Be careful with your words, my son, and try to understand what God is, what the world is, and what it means for something to be immortal or subject to dissolution. Know that the world exists within God, just as God exists within everything. Humans, however, belong to the world and exist within it.

God is the beginning, the end, and the essence of everything that exists.

The Seventeenth Book,
To Asclepius, To Be Truly Wise

Since Tat, my son, was eager to learn about the nature of all things, he didn't allow me to stop teaching him. Although he was young, he was determined to understand every detail, so I had to explain many things in depth to make his learning smoother and more successful. But with you, I will keep it brief, focusing only on the essential points. I will also interpret these ideas more deeply, as you have both the wisdom and the years to grasp the true nature of things.

Everything we see has been created and is continually being created. However, nothing creates itself. Every created thing comes from something else. There are many different kinds of things in the world, each distinct from the other. If all things are made by another, there must be one being who creates everything—someone who was never created but is older than all else. This creator, being unmade, is more ancient than anything that has ever come into existence.

He is the most powerful, the one who knows all things, and nothing existed before him. He governs both the great and small, controlling the variety of everything that exists. His power holds everything together and keeps the process of creation ongoing. The things that are made are visible, but the maker remains invisible. He creates everything to make his presence known, and because of this, he continues to create endlessly.

Understanding this fills the soul with admiration and gratitude. Knowing your divine creator is the greatest blessing, for what could be sweeter than knowing your true father? But who is this being, and how can we recognize him? Should we call him God, the Maker, or the Father—or perhaps all three? We call him God because of his power, the Maker because of his creative work, and the Father because of his goodness.

His power is beyond the things he has made, but through his actions, all things are brought into being. So, instead of engaging in endless debate, we must focus on understanding two truths: the one who creates and the things that are created. Nothing exists outside of these two realities, and nothing stands between them.

Remember this: all things boil down to these two truths—the maker and the creation—and one cannot exist without the other. The creator needs the creation to express his nature, and the creation needs the creator to exist. They are inseparably united, like two parts of the same whole.

Since the creator is complete in himself, everything he makes reflects his essence. That which is made exists because the creator wills it to be. Without the creator, nothing could exist, and without creation, the creator's work would be incomplete. So, creation follows the creator, and in this way, they are joined as one. God is the one who creates, and all that is created follows his design.

We should not fear the variety of things in the world, nor think that it reflects poorly on the creator. Instead, it glorifies him, for it is through creating all things that he expresses his greatness. Creation is like the body of God, and in this divine work, there is nothing shameful or wrong. Just as rust forms naturally on copper, or waste emerges from the body, certain things are simply a result of the process of generation.

The rust is not created by the blacksmith, nor is waste created by the body itself. Similarly, God does not create evil. These imperfections arise naturally from the cycles of life. Change is necessary, like the cleansing that keeps the process of creation in motion.

Consider a painter who creates both the heavens and the earth, gods and humans, animals, and plants. If a painter can create all these things, why would it be hard to imagine that God creates everything? It is foolish to think otherwise. Those who deny this are trapped in ignorance. They claim to praise God but refuse to acknowledge him as the creator of all things, which is both absurd and impious.

By denying God's role in creation, they attribute human flaws like pride, weakness, or envy to him. This is deeply misguided, for God is none of these things. His only quality is goodness. Being good, he lacks pride, ignorance, or malice. God is pure goodness itself.

Because God is good, he has the power to create all things. Everything that exists comes from the Good. Just as a farmer sows seeds in different places—wheat in one spot, barley in another, and vines elsewhere—God also plants seeds of immortality in the world. Through him, life, change, and motion exist.

In truth, there are only a few key elements in all of existence: God, generation, and the life force that animates everything. In these, all things are contained.

Thank you for Reading

You've Just Read a Piece of the Greatest Library Ever Rebuilt

Thank you for reading.

This book is one of thousands we're restoring, reimagining, and translating as part of the **Modern Library of Alexandria** — a global movement to preserve and share humanity's most important ideas.

What was once lost to fire and time is now rising again — not just as memory, but as living, breathing knowledge, freely accessible to all.

What You Can Do Next:

- **Keep Reading.**

  Discover more legendary works — in beautiful print, audiobook, or digital form — at LibraryofAlexandria.com.

- **Build Your Own Library.**

  Every title is available as a paperback, hardcover, or collectible boxset — at true printing cost. Craft a personal library worthy of display.

- **Spread the Light.**

  Share this book. Tell others about the movement. Help us translate every timeless work into every language, so no reader is ever left behind.

By finishing this book, you've already taken part in something extraordinary.

Join us at LibraryofAlexandria.com

Together, we're rebuilding the greatest library the world has ever known.

With appreciation,
The Modern Library of Alexandria Team

Visit:

www.libraryofalexandria.com

Or scan the code below: